# COOKING WITH THE CRUNCH BROS

# COOKING
## WITH THE CRUNCH
# BROS

Casual and Fun
Korean- and
Japanese-Inspired
Recipes from Our
Kitchen to Yours

**By Jeff
& Jordan Kim,
The CrunchBros**

**(With Lots of Help
from CrunchMom)**

HARVARD
COMMON
PRESS

**Quarto.com**

© 2023 Quarto Publishing Group USA Inc.
Text © 2023 The CrunchFamily LLC
Photography © 2023 David K. Peng

First Published in 2023 by The Harvard Common Press, an imprint of The Quarto Group,
100 Cummings Center, Suite 265-D, Beverly, MA 01915, USA.
T (978) 282-9590 F (978) 283-2742

The Harvard Common Press titles are also available at discount for retail, wholesale, promotional, and bulk purchase.
For details, contact the Special Sales Manager by email at specialsales@quarto.com or by mail at The Quarto Group,
Attn: Special Sales Manager, 100 Cummings Center, Suite 265-D, Beverly, MA 01915, USA.

27 26 25 24 23     1 2 3 4 5

ISBN: 978-0-7603-8523-4

Digital edition published in 2023
eISBN: 978-0-7603-8524-1

Library of Congress Cataloging-in-Publication Data available

Design: Burge Agency
Photography: David K. Peng
Food Stylist: Christiane Hur

Printed in China

This book is dedicated to you, our CrunchFam. When we say we couldn't have done this without all of you, we 100% mean it. Thank you for your support over the last few years. Thank you for laughing with us, for sticking with us, and for always helping us share some positivity in this world. We love you guys. Thank you. Gamsahapnida. Arigatou. Mahalo. Oh, and LET'S EAT!

PLEASE SCAN THIS QR CODE TO SEE A SPECIAL MESSAGE WE CREATED FOR YOU. IT'S DEDICATED TO ALL OF YOU WHO HAVE THIS BOOK.

# CONTENTS

# INTRODUCTION

## *JAL MEOKGETSEUBNIDA!*
## *ITADAKIMASU!*
## LET'S EAT!

Whoa! Check it out! We wrote a cookbook! Are we super excited about this?! Yes! Are we professional chefs? Nope. But do we love to cook and eat? Absolutely! Our entire family has a passion for food, for cooking, and for trying new things. Whenever we're not making *mukbangs* we're in the kitchen cooking up our snacks and meals.

And now we're glad you're here with us. We say *Jal meokgetseubnida!* and *Itadakimasu!* to you to welcome you to our table. We're a Korean–American family on CrunchDad's side and a Japanese-American family on CrunchMom's side, and those expressions mean "I will eat well" and "thank you for this meal" in, respectively, Korean and Japanese.

Why did we write this book, you ask? We wrote this book with all of you in mind. We wrote it in hopes of getting more people to try different things, experience our cultures, and to just have fun in the kitchen. We also hope that our recipes help you decide what to make for dinner. Because face it, trying to figure out what to make every night can be a pain.

As we mentioned above, our family created this cookbook with everybody in mind. Our recipes are pretty much for everyone and anyone who enjoys cooking or wants to take a stab in the kitchen. Whether you're cooking for yourself, your mom, your child, or your entire family, we hope we've got you covered!

You know how we said we weren't chefs? That was only partially true. The truth is, the two grown-ups here, CrunchDad (CD) and CrunchMom (CM), have a pretty extensive history in the restaurant industry. We even started and ran our own pop-up

## A MESSAGE FROM JORDAN

Hello everyone! Thank you for watching our videos and commenting and liking them. So, we're making a CrunchBros cookbook. I hope you use our cookbook to cook our favorite dishes! Don't forget to keep trying new foods! Thank you!

## A MESSAGE FROM CRUNCHDAD

What's up everyone! Thank you for your support and for really caring about our CrunchFamily.

I can't express how much I appreciate all of you. Starting The CrunchBros has been such an amazing journey. I could've never imagined we would be here publishing a cookbook and being able to share some of our favorite recipes! This has all been made possible because of you guys, and we truly are blessed to have you all in our lives. Thank you all! Welcome to the CrunchFamily!

Hawaii slinging kimchi, yakisoba, and more. We brought the best of both our worlds, Korean and Japanese, together and created dishes from our own cultures like Korean-style pork belly kimchi and Japanese-style coffee jelly. We also served up a lot of fusion plates, one of the most popular being our pork belly kimchi sliders on a sweet roll with guava sauce—whoa, was that ever good! Anyway, later on we created awesome fusion kids, too, but that storyline is for another time.

Let's introduce ourselves to the ones who are just joining in.

Who are The CrunchBros? We're a father-son duo, Jeff Kim the dad and Jordan Kim the son, who create fun and wholesome videos on social media. We first started off doing ASMR videos and mukbangs where we would try new foods and local dishes. We started these videos when Jordan was three years old, and a goal of ours is to have him keep trying new foods. We want our kids to be exposed to different cultures and foods and to see what's out there.

We didn't realize how great of a learning experience this would become for him as well as for the rest of us. We've since been creating lots of recipe videos as well as sharing travel and life experiences. You can join us on our adventures on YouTube,

TikTok, Instagram, and Facebook @thecrunchbros.

This book may be The CrunchBros cookbook, but The CrunchBros is actually a family entity: one that would not exist without each and every member of our home.

First up, there's Jeff, a.k.a. CrunchDad. He's best known for his insatiable appetite and love for spicy food. CrunchDad is his name and hot sauce is his game. As much as he loves to eat, he loves to cook. CrunchDad grew up cooking in the kitchen at a very young age. His mother was a stay-at-home mom and would cook meals every day. He grew up watching and learning how to

JEFF, A.K.A. CRUNCHDAD

JORDAN, A.K.A. THE CRUNCHBRO

CRUNCHMOM, A.K.A. CRUNCHBOSS

KAIYA, A.K.A. CRUNCHBABY

## A MESSAGE FROM CRUNCHMOM

*Konnichiwa* everyone! First of all, I want to say thank you—thank you—thank you from the bottom of my heart. What a crazy journey we have been on, and to have all of you alongside us through it all has been amazing. If anyone had told me a few years ago that we would be creating a cookbook, I would've told them to shut the front door. I hope you enjoy and have fun with our recipes as much as we do. These are just a few of our favorites that we like to make in our home, and we hope some of them will become your favorites too. Enjoy!

## A MESSAGE FROM KAIYA (KIND OF)

Buru buru buru buru!

This is Kaiya's signature sign-off at the end of her videos. Do we know what it means? No.

---

create Korean dishes like *kimchi jjigae* (kimchi stew) and *miyeokguk* (seaweed soup, traditionally eaten on birthdays). To this day, the kitchen is his comfort zone, a place where he enjoys being and where he loves to create dishes for his family.

Next up is Jordan, the brightest and sassiest kid with the biggest personality that we know. He is THE CrunchBro. He's best known for giving CrunchDad a hard time and perfecting the art of the side eye. If there was a Guinness World Record for being able to take the Biggest-Small bites, Jordan would be your man. He's also a whiz in the kitchen. He's been helping make meals and even creating ones of his own ever since he was three years old. He is a self-proclaimed

"Flip Master." He can flip pancakes and *okonomiyaki* (Japanese savory pancakes) like it's no one's business. As his parents, one of the most commonly asked questions we get is: How do you get Jordan to be such an adventurous eater? It's hard to pinpoint one thing, but we do believe that him being so hands-on in the kitchen since an early age has definitely helped. A big thing we encourage is not to give up if your child doesn't care for a certain food. Taste buds are always evolving. There are foods that Jordan used to hate a few years ago, but now loves, and vice versa. He used to love blueberries, but now refuses to go anywhere near them. The point is, don't give up on a food just because you or your child doesn't like it. They might end up liking it in a few months or even

after a year or two. We asked Jordan a little while ago why he likes trying new things. He answered, "How else would I know what it tastes like?!" Touché, Jordan, touché.

Then there's Kaiya, a.k.a. CrunchBaby. She's our wild and carefree daughter who keeps everyone around her in check. She'll eat and try anything we throw her way and is able to out-eat any small human. She's like a walking, talking, living vacuum, and we love it. It's hard to believe, but she loves fruits and veggies over most foods. If there's a plate of string beans at the table, good luck trying to get one before she finishes it all. Recently, she has become really interested in helping out in the kitchen just like her big brother. They sometimes tag-team and

# LET'S GET COOKING.

create little snacks or dishes for us. As parents, it's one of the sweetest things to see. We love watching our kids having fun in the kitchen.

Next up is CrunchMom, a.k.a. CrunchBoss. She works her magic from behind the scenes and keeps everyone in line. She's known most for her sassy comments and for roasting CrunchDad in all the mukbangs. If sass is a genetic trait, we all know where Jordan got his from. Growing up in a Japanese household and having an amazing mom who is an awesome cook helped shape her love and passion for food. When it comes to food,

most of her childhood memories are of her mom's home-cooked meals. In grade school, teachers would come out every day during lunch time to see what her mom packed for her in her bento. Every day would be a different lunch. Her bento boxes would be two-tiered and include items like *tamagoyaki* (Japanese rolled omelet), *onigiri*, *kinpira* (braised vegetables in sugar, soy sauce, mirin, and sake), and so much more. As a young, introverted kid, it was embarrassing at times to get that much attention, but looking back now, OMG, what a crazy flex that was.

That last story segues right into CrunchMom's mom, a.k.a. Baba, a.k.a. Jordan and Kaiya's Grandma. Baba has been such a huge influence in our kids' lives. She's the real MVP. She's the silent assassin who slays in the kitchen and makes it look too easy. Having been born and raised in Japan, her cooking revolves around Japanese food. A lot of Jordan's and CrunchMom's recipes have either come from Baba or have been inspired by her. Blessed is an understatement when it comes to having Baba in our home.

# CHAPTER 1

# EASY PEASY SIDES, SNACKS, AND SAUCES

1

# SPICY TOFU

This is an easy recipe that takes tofu up a notch. It's a little sweet and a little spicy and can be eaten hot or cold.

1. Cut the tofu into 1-inch (2.5 cm) squares with ¼-inch (6 mm) thickness. You should be able to get 16 squares total.

2. Heat a large frying pan on high and add 1 tablespoon (15 ml) of sesame oil. Once the oil is hot, add the tofu squares and cook on each side till they become nice and golden brown.

3. While the tofu cooks, add the ingredients for the sauce to a small mixing bowl and combine until the sugar has dissolved.

4. Once the tofu is done, add the sauce and cook for 5 minutes on medium.

1 package (19 ounces, or 562 g) firm tofu

1 tablespoon (15 ml) sesame oil

**SAUCE**

1 tablespoon (15 ml) sesame oil

2 tablespoons (28 ml) soy sauce

¼ cup (60 ml) water

2 tablespoons (26 g) Korean chili flakes

2 garlic cloves, minced

1 tablespoon (13 g) sugar

1 tablespoon (8 g) roasted sesame seeds

¼ cup (25 g) green onions, thinly sliced

# TOFU "STEAK"

Our kids absolutely love this, and it's good any time of the day. We make it as part of our breakfast, lunch, or dinner—it all works!

1. Take the tofu out of the package and wrap it in a paper towel. Let it sit for 1 hour or longer on top of a cooling rack (make sure to have something to catch the excess liquid underneath).

2. After draining, cut into 1-inch (2.5 cm) squares with ¼-inch (6 mm) thickness. You should be able to get about 16 squares total.

3. Pat the tofu dry with a paper towel to get rid of excess water.

4. Heat a large frying pan on high and add the oil. Once the oil is hot, add the tofu slices and cook on both sides until golden brown (about 2 minutes each side).

5. Add the soy sauce, mirin, and green onions to the pan.

6. Cook the tofu for an additional 1–2 minutes on each side.

1 package (19 ounces, or 540 g) medium-firm to firm tofu

1½ tablespoons (25 ml) neutral oil

2½ tablespoons (38 ml) soy sauce

1 tablespoon (15 ml) mirin

2 green onion stalks, minced

**TIP:**
If you don't drain enough of the water from the tofu, it will dilute the flavor.

# MARINATED SOY SAUCE EGGS

Once you start eating these, you're never going to go back to regular hard-boiled eggs. This recipe will get you hooked.

1. Bring a large pot of water to a boil. Once it's at a rolling boil, add the eggs and cook for 7 minutes.

2. While the eggs are boiling, add all the ingredients for the marinade to a large, lidded container. Mix well and set aside.

3. Remove the eggs, place into an ice bath (cold water and ice), and let sit for 5 minutes. This will make it easier to peel the eggs.

4. Once the eggs have cooled, peel and place into the marinade. Let the eggs marinate overnight in the fridge and then enjoy!

**TIP:**
A 7-minute egg will give you a jammy center. If you like your eggs more well-done, boil them for a few extra minutes.

6 large eggs

**MARINADE**

½ cup (120 ml) soy sauce

3 tablespoons (45 ml) white vinegar

3 garlic cloves, chopped

¼ cup (25 g) green onion, thinly sliced

1 tablespoon (15 ml) sesame oil

2 tablespoons (16 g) roasted sesame seeds

2 Thai chile peppers (or any chile pepper you like—spice it up!)

¼ cup (60 ml) water

¼ cup (50 g) sugar

1 tablespoon (13 g) Korean chili flakes

# KIMCHI MAC SALAD

CrunchMom and I came up with this recipe while living in Hawaii. We took the classic mac salad and added a twist. Whoever says that kimchi makes everything better . . . is absolutely right.

1. Cook the macaroni following the instructions on the package.

2. While that's cooking, chop the kimchi and dice up the deli ham.

3. Drain the macaroni and run under cold water.

4. Add the drained macaroni to a large mixing bowl. Add the kimchi, deli ham, and all the remaining ingredients to the macaroni and mix thoroughly.

5. Refrigerate till you are ready to serve.

8 ounces (225 g) macaroni

2 cups (200 g) kimchi

6 ounces (170 g) deli ham

½ cup (60 g) thinly sliced cucumber

½ cup (61 g) thinly sliced carrots

¼ cup (58 g) thinly sliced onions

1 small apple, thinly sliced

1¼ cups (285 g) Japanese mayo

¼ cup (60 ml) milk

2 tablespoons (26 g) Korean chili flakes (optional)

Black pepper to taste

# SESAME ZUCCHINI

Here's a simple and healthy side dish that's easy to get on board with that's a favorite of our little one, Kaiya. She loves anything with veggies.

1. Heat a large frying pan on high. Add all the ingredients and cook for 5–8 minutes, stirring occasionally.

2. Remove from the pan and garnish with sesame seeds and green onions.

2 cups (240 g) zucchini, cut into ¼-inch (6 mm) slices (rounds or half-moon shapes)

1 tablespoon (15 ml) sesame oil

Black pepper to taste

1 tablespoon (13 g) Korean chili flakes

¼ teaspoon beef stock powder

Roasted sesame seeds for garnish

Green onions, thinly sliced, for garnish

# CORN CHEESE

One of the most popular side dishes served along Korean BBQ is the corn cheese. It's corn and cheese—you can't ever go wrong with that combo.

1. Drain the canned corn.

2. Add the corn, ½ cup (58 g) of mozzarella cheese, mayo, salt, pepper, and garlic powder to a large mixing bowl and mix thoroughly.

3. Spread the mixture into a baking dish and sprinkle the remaining ½ cup (58 g) of mozzarella cheese and dried parsley over top.

4. Bake in the oven at 425°F (220°C, or gas mark 7) for 20–25 minutes.

1 can (15.7 ounces, or 445 g) corn

1 cup (115 g) shredded mozzarella cheese (or your favorite cheese blend)

3 tablespoons (42 g) Japanese mayo

Salt to taste

Black pepper to taste

¼ teaspoon garlic powder

¼ teaspoon dried parsley

# MISO CORN

Our whole family loves all things corn and no matter how many of these ears we make, there's always a battle for the last one.

1. Mix the miso and mayo and then spread it onto the corn.

2. Sprinkle the shredded cheese on top. Use as much or as little cheese as you like.

3. Air fry for 8–10 minutes at 350°F (180°C, or gas mark 4). If you don't have an air fryer, you can also bake them in the oven at 350°F (180°C, or gas mark 4) for about 10–15 minutes.

4 teaspoons (21 g) miso

4 teaspoons (19 g) Japanese mayo

4 ears corn

4 tablespoons (30 g) shredded cheese (your favorite blend)

# SWEET AND SPICY CAULIFLOWER

Here's a recipe that takes a lackluster vegetable like cauliflower and jazzes it up with some in-your-face flavor.

1 head cauliflower

**SAUCE**

1 tablespoon (22 g) gochujang

5 tablespoons (75 g) ketchup

3 tablespoons (39 g) sugar

3 tablespoons (64 g) corn syrup

2 tablespoons (28 ml) soy sauce

1 tablespoon (13 g) Korean chili flakes

1 tablespoon (8 g) roasted sesame seeds

1. Cut the cauliflower into bite-size pieces and steam until tender. Set it aside and make sure it is completely dry before adding it to the sauce later.

2. Heat a large frying pan on medium-high. Add all the ingredients for the sauce to the pan and combine.

3. Once the sauce is thoroughly mixed, add in the steamed cauliflower, stirring to coat each piece, about 5 minutes.

4. Garnish with more sesame seeds and serve hot.

# SPICY MU

## (SPICY DAIKON)

This is a great *banchan*, or side dish, we make whenever we're doing Korean BBQ at home. It's spicy, a little sweet, and goes really well rolled up in a lettuce leaf with some meat and rice.

1. Cut the daikon into ½-inch (1.3 cm) cubes.

2. Salt the daikon cubes, let sit for about 15 minutes in a large mixing bowl, and then rinse, making sure to wash off all the salt.

3. Set the daikon cubes aside and let drain.

4. While you wait, cut the chives into 2-inch (2.5 cm) segments and place into a large mixing bowl.

5. Add all the remaining ingredients and mix well.

6. Let sit in the fridge for a few hours or overnight. These are best if eaten within 1 week.

1 pound (455 g) daikon (approximately)

2 tablespoons (36 g) salt

½ pound (225 g) chives

3 tablespoons (39 g) Korean chili flakes

2 tablespoons (26 g) sugar

4 garlic cloves, minced

1 tablespoon (15 ml) sesame oil

1 tablespoon (15 ml) rice vinegar

# SHOYU MAYO ASPARAGUS

Kaiya goes to town on this asparagus dish whenever we cook them up. She'll finish these before she moves onto anything else on her plate. *Shoyu* means soy sauce in Japanese.

1 pound (455 g) asparagus

1 tablespoon (15 ml) soy sauce

2 tablespoons (28 g) Japanese mayo (You can definitely add more if you're feeling it.)

Bonito flakes for garnish

1. Cut about ½ inch (1.3 cm) off the bottom of the asparagus stalks.

2. Heat water to a boil in either in a large frying pan or pot and boil the asparagus for 2–3 minutes.

3. Drain the asparagus and place into an 11- × 7-inch (28 × 18 cm) baking dish.

4. Mix in the soy sauce, making sure to coat the asparagus evenly. Squeeze the mayo over top in a zigzag pattern.

5. Bake the asparagus at 350°F (180°C, or gas mark 4) for about 10 minutes.

6. Sprinkle with the bonito flakes and enjoy.

**TIP:**
Make sure not to overcook or boil the asparagus so you have a nice little crunch and snap to it after it's baked.

# QUICK SWEET AND SPICY CUCUMBER

This is our take on cucumber kimchi. It's quick, easy, and gives you a satisfying crunch.

1. Cut the cucumber into ½-inch (1.3 cm) circles.

2. Salt the cucumber slices, let sit for about 15 minutes, and then rinse, making sure to wash off all of the salt.

3. Pat the cucumber slices dry and place into a large mixing bowl.

4. Add all the remaining ingredients. Mix well and let it sit in the fridge for a few hours or overnight.

1 pound (455 g) Persian cucumbers

2 tablespoons (36 g) salt

2 tablespoons (26 g) Korean chili flakes

1½ tablespoons (20 g) sugar

3 garlic cloves, minced

1 tablespoon (15 ml) sesame oil

2 tablespoons (16 g) roasted sesame seeds

1 tablespoon (15 ml) rice vinegar

# CHOP, CHOP, CHOP

# DAIKON AND CARROTS

The kids eat these sweet and sour pickles in all different ways—as a snack, as a topper for sandwiches, tucked inside a lettuce wrap with meat—you name it!

1. Combine the sugar, vinegar, water, and salt in a small mixing bowl.

2. Whisk until the sugar and salt have completely dissolved.

3. Next, peel and cut the carrots and daikon into 3- to 4-inch (7.5 to 10 cm) sticks.

4. Place the carrot and daikon sticks into a lidded container and cover with the vinegar mixture.

5. Let this marinade overnight in the fridge and enjoy the next day.

¼ cup (50 g) sugar

¼ cup (60 ml) white vinegar

½ cup (120 ml) warm water

¼ teaspoon salt

1 carrot (5 ounces, 142 g)

1 daikon (5 ounces, 142 g)

# KIMCHI PICO DE GALLO

Here's another recipe we came up when we were living in Hawaii. It was a major hit *there*, and so we wanted to share it with you *here*.

1. Add all the ingredients to a large mixing bowl.

2. Once thoroughly mixed, place into the fridge for 1 to 3 hours to set and enjoy!

2 cups (360 g) diced tomatoes

1 cup (160 g) diced onions

1 cup (100 g) diced kimchi

1 cup (16 g) cilantro, chopped

4 tablespoons (60 ml) lime juice

Salt to taste

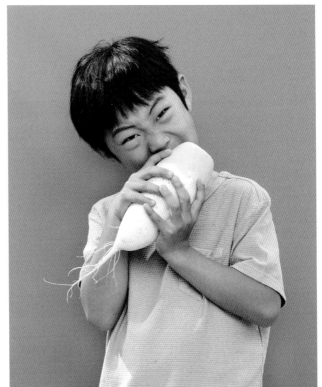

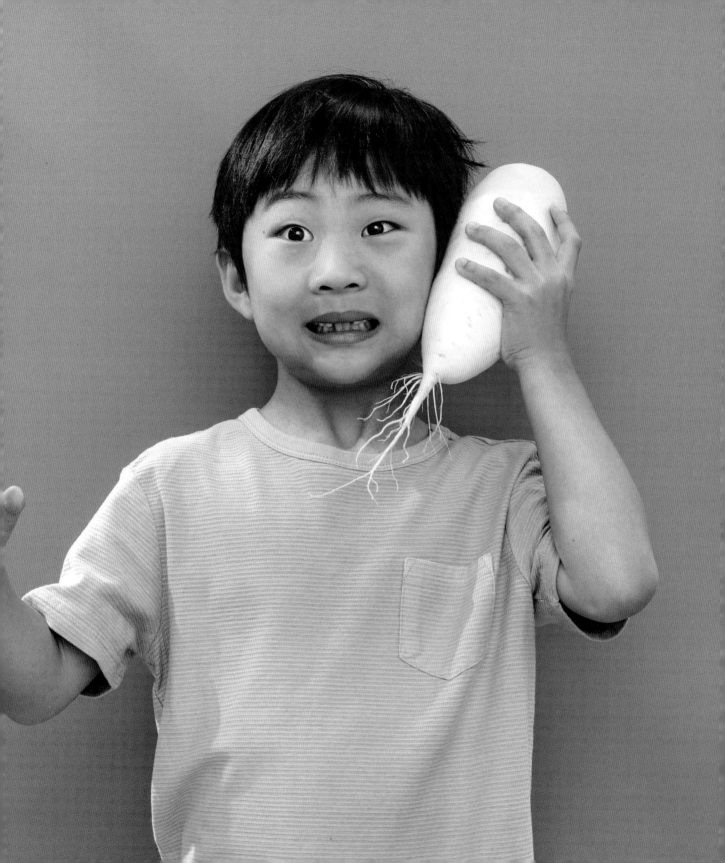

# KIMCHI GUAC

This recipe started off with avocado toast in mind. But it turned out so good, the toast got ditched, and it transformed into a kimchi guacamole instead.

1. Dice the avocados and kimchi. You can mash up the avocados or you can leave them diced— it's totally up to you.

2. Add all the ingredients to a large mixing bowl and combine.

3. Salt to taste and then serve.

2 avocados

½ cup (50 g) kimchi

1 tablespoon (13 g) Korean chili flakes

2 tablespoons (28 g) Japanese mayo

¼ cup (4 g) cilantro, chopped

Salt to taste

# MISO MAYO DIP

If you need help eating your veggies, this dip is your answer. Grab your favorite and not so favorite veggies and dab them in this dip. You'll thank us later.

1. Combine all the ingredients together in a small mixing bowl.

2. Store in an airtight container in the refrigerator for up to 3 days.

1 tablespoon (16 g) miso

½ cup (112 g) Japanese mayo

½ tablespoon mirin

1½ teaspoons roasted sesame seeds

# GALBI MARINADE

We're sharing our go-to *galbi*, or Korean short rib, marinade. It's not only great for short ribs, but it's also awesome with pork belly.

1. Place all the ingredients except for the sesame oil, pepper, and sesame seeds into a blender and blend until smooth.

2. Pour out into a large mixing bowl and add the sesame oil, pepper, and sesame seeds and whisk well. This will marinade up to 24 ounces (680 g) of protein of your choice. You can use the marinade immediately or refrigerate and use the next day.

3. Marinate your protein choice for at least 2–4 hours in the fridge.

⅔ cup (160 ml) soy sauce

½ cup (120 ml) water

⅔ cup (133 g) sugar

3 tablespoons (45 ml) mirin

1 Asian pear or 2 apples (if you can't find an Asian pear)

1 small onion

1 piece (¼ inch, or 6 mm) fresh ginger

½ cup (25 g) green onions, thinly sliced

4 tablespoons (60 ml) sesame oil

Black pepper to taste

4 tablespoons (32 g) roasted sesame seeds

# SOY-VINEGAR DIPPING SAUCE

This is a great dipping sauce for *mandu*, Korean dumplings, or *pajeon*, Korean pancakes. The vinegariness really helps cut the grease of a dish.

1. Add all the ingredients to a large mixing bowl and mix thoroughly.

4 tablespoons (60 ml) soy sauce

2 tablespoons (28 ml) white vinegar

1 tablespoon (13 g) Korean chili flakes

1 tablespoon (15 ml) sesame oil

1 tablespoon (6 g) thinly sliced green onion

# WHAT'S UP CRUNCHFAM?

# GOCHUJANG DIPPING SAUCE

This gochujang dipping sauce is a popular sauce that Koreans eat with their sushi. It's sweet, spicy, and vinegary.

2 tablespoons (44 g) gochujang

2 tablespoons (28 ml) white vinegar

1 tablespoon (13 g) sugar

1. Add all the ingredients to a small mixing bowl and mix until the sugar has dissolved completely.

# YAKINIKU SAUCE

*Yakiniku* is typically grilled meat, but we use this sauce to add flavor to our fried rice, tofu, veggies, and more.

1. Combine all the ingredients together in a medium mixing bowl.

2. Store in an airtight container in the refrigerator for 5 to 7 days.

1⅓ cups (133 g) thinly sliced green onions

5 teaspoons (13 g) roasted sesame seeds

⅓ cup (67 g) sugar

1 cup (235 ml) soy sauce

2 tablespoons (28 ml) cooking sake

1 teaspoon black pepper

2–3 garlic cloves, grated

1 teaspoon lemon juice

# IN THE KITCHEN WITH CRUNCHDAD

2

# COLD NOODS THAT BRING THE HEAT

A perfect dish on a hot day, these cold noods bring about the right amount of heat and crunch. We always have these ingredients on hand, so I definitely make this often during the summer.

1. Cook the somen following the instructions on the package.

2. While the somen cooks, shred the imitation crab and cut the cucumber and takuwan into matchstick pieces.

3. Once the somen are done, run them under cold water.

4. Let drain and then portion into 4 bowls. Divide all the remaining ingredients and place on top of the somen. Add gochujang to taste.

16 ounces (455 g) somen

8 ounces (225 g) imitation crab

8 ounces (225 g) cucumber

8 ounces (225 g) takuwan

2 ounces (55 g) green onion, thinly sliced

8 ounces (225 g) kimchi

4 tablespoons (60 ml) sesame oil

Gochujang to taste

# BLACK BEAN NOODS
## (JJAJANGMYEON)

Jjajangmyeon is one of my go-to noodle dishes. Jordan and I do a lot of mukbangs eating this, and we even made this on our YouTube page a while back. It's a classic dish and definitely one of my comfort foods.

1. Heat a large frying pan on high and add the oil. Once the oil is hot, add the black bean paste. You want to stir and cook this paste in the oil for 2–3 minutes (this will help reduce any bitter flavors). Remove from the pan and set aside.

2. Next, add the veggies, minced garlic, and pork belly and cook for 5 minutes or until the pork is golden brown and crispy.

3. Add the water and bring to a boil. Once it comes to a boil, add the cooked black bean paste and lower the heat to a simmer.

4. At this point, you can add a cornstarch slurry if you want your sauce to be thicker. Simmer for 10–15 minutes and then it's ready.

5. Serve over the cooked jjajangmyeon noodles.

2 tablespoons (28 ml) neutral oil

3 tablespoons (57 g) black bean paste

¾ cup (120 g) diced onions

½ cup (60 g) zucchini, cut into ½-inch (1.3 cm) cubes

½ cup (55 g) potato, cut into ½-inch (1.3 cm) cubes

5 garlic cloves, minced

8 ounces (225 g) pork belly, cut into ½-inch (1.3 cm) cubes

1½ cups (355 ml) water

Cornstarch slurry, 1 tablespoon (8 g) cornstarch plus 1 tablespoon (15 ml) water (optional)

28 ounces (795 g) fresh jjajangmyeon noodles, cooked

**TIP:**
If you don't have access to fresh Jjajangmyeon noodles, dried noodles work too.

# MACBOKKI

This is mac n' cheese but with a Korean twist. We replaced the macaroni with tteok, creating a cheesy, chewy, and delicious dish.

1. Preheat the oven to 450°F (250°C, or gas mark 8).

2. Heat a large frying pan on medium and melt the butter. Pour in the milk and stir to combine. Add the seasonings and mix well. Gradually add in three quarters of the shredded cheese and stir to completely melt the cheese.

3. Place the tteok in the bottom of a 9- × 13-inch (23 cm × 33 cm) baking dish. Pour in the cheese sauce and mix thoroughly, spreading evenly. Top with the remaining shredded cheese. Place the baking dish into the middle of the oven and bake for 20–25 minutes.

4. When it's finished, give it a good stir before serving.

4 tablespoons (55 g) butter

2 cups (475 ml) milk

2 garlic cloves, minced

1 teaspoon beef stock powder

Salt to taste

Black pepper to taste

½ teaspoon garlic powder

½ teaspoon onion powder

2 cups (230 g) shredded cheese (your favorite blend)

2 pounds (900 g) tteok

**TIP:**
For an extra crunch, you can sprinkle ½ cup (56 g) of panko over the top before placing into the oven.

# KOREAN BREAKFAST BURRITO

I'm a sucker for a good breakfast burrito, so adding some heat to it was a no-brainer. I eat this for breakfast, brunch, lunch, snack, and dinner. You name it—it's good anytime of the day.

16 ounces (455 g) bacon

4 large eggs

½ tablespoon Korean chili flakes

½ teaspoon beef stock powder

2 tablespoons (28 g) butter

8 tablespoons (60 g) shredded cheese (your favorite blend)

½ tablespoon gochujang

2 tablespoons (28 g) Japanese mayo

4 large tortillas

1. Cook the bacon in a large frying pan over medium-high heat and set aside.

2. Crack the eggs into a large mixing bowl and add the Korean chili flakes and beef stock powder. Whisk to combine.

3. Heat a large pan on high. Pour in the egg mixture and scramble. Add the bacon once the eggs are done and remove from the heat.

4. Combine the gochujang and mayo to create the sauce that goes into the burritos.

5. Take a large tortilla, add the desired amount of the gochujang mayo, and spread it evenly. Next, sprinkle in some shredded cheese and add the eggs and bacon mixture on top.

6. Roll up the burrito and enjoy.

**TIPS:**

- Toast your burrito on a frying pan for a few minutes for some crunch.

- Add some Kimchi Guac (see page 44) and Kimchi Pico de Gallo (see page 41) to level up your breakfast even more!

# NOT SO SWEET SAVORY KOREAN PANCAKES

What's great about these pancakes is that you can add different ingredients to keep everyone happy. Jordan loves his with seafood, Kaiya loves hers with mushrooms, CrunchMom and Baba always stick with kimchi, and my favorite has to be the classic green onion.

1 cup (125 g) all-purpose flour

3 tablespoons (36 g) potato starch

1 teaspoon beef stock powder

1½ cups (355 ml) water

¾ cup (120 g) sliced onions

8 stalks chopped green onion

2 large eggs

8 ounces (225 g) cooked meat of choice (optional)

3 tablespoons (45 ml) neutral oil

1. Add all the ingredients except for the oil to a large mixing bowl. Combine until everything is well incorporated.

2. Heat a medium-sized frying pan on medium to high and add the oil. When the oil is hot, ladle the pancake mixture into the pan. Cook for about 5 minutes or until golden brown and then flip. Cook until both sides are nice and golden brown and serve hot.

3. Repeat with the remaining batter.

**TIP:**
This pairs great with the Soy-Vinegar Dipping Sauce on page 47.

# KIMBAP

*Kimbap* is like a one-stop shop for a meal. You get your protein, your carbs, and your veggies all in one roll. I also love how great these are to take out with you when you're on the go. We've taken these to the park, road trips, on the plane, and even on boat rides (the family surprised me one year on Father's Day with a boat ride, and we took these bad boys with us).

1 medium-sized carrot

2 teaspoons sesame oil, divided

8 ounces (225 g) spinach

2 large eggs

¼ teaspoon salt

4 nori sheets

4 cups (744 g) cooked rice

8 ounces (225 g) takuwan

8 ounces (225 g) bulgogi

Roasted sesame seeds for garnish

1. Cut the carrots into matchsticks.

2. Heat a medium-sized frying pan on medium. Add 1 teaspoon of sesame oil, carrots, and salt to taste. Cook the carrots until tender. Remove from the pan and set aside to cool.

3. Using the same pan, add 1 teaspoon of sesame oil, spinach, and salt to taste. Cook the spinach for 3 minutes or until completely wilted. Remove the spinach to a colander and let drain and cool.

4. Next, whisk the eggs and add a pinch of salt. Add a thin layer of egg into the pan. Flip once and cook until set. Then remove from the pan and place onto a cutting board. Repeat until all the egg mixture is cooked. Once the eggs have cooled, cut into ½-inch (1.3 cm) strips and set aside.

5. Take a full sheet of nori and place it on a cutting board. Take the rice and spread a thin layer to cover the entire surface of the nori. Next, start placing each desired item lengthwise across the middle of the rice. Roll from one end to the other, making sure to roll it into a tight cylinder.

6. Serve whole or cut into 8 pieces. Garnish with sesame seeds.

# BIBIMBAP

As seen in a lot of Korean television dramas, *bibimbap* is a classic. I personally appreciate this meal because you can basically throw in whatever you have in the fridge and call it a day. Get creative with the ingredients. You can add tuna, *bulgogi*, fish cakes the list goes on and on!

1. Cut the carrots into matchsticks.

2. Heat a medium-sized frying pan on medium. Add 1 teaspoon of sesame oil, carrots, and salt to taste. Cook the carrots until tender. Remove from the pan and set aside to cool. Repeat the same process for the bean sprouts.

3. In the same pan, add 1 teaspoon of sesame oil, spinach, and salt to taste. Cook the spinach for 3 minutes or until wilted. Remove the spinach to a colander and let drain and cool.

4. Cook your choice of meat.

5. Cook 4 sunny-side up eggs and set aside.

6. Portion out the rice into 4 bowls. Divide all the cooked ingredients and place on top of the rice, making sure to add the eggs last. Drizzle with a small amount of sesame oil, sprinkle some sesame seeds over top, and add gochujang to taste.

1 large carrot

1 tablespoon (15 ml) sesame oil, divided

8 ounces (225 g) bean sprouts

8 ounces (225 g) spinach

12 ounces (340 g) meat of choice

4 large eggs

4 cups (744 g) cooked rice

¼ teaspoon salt

Roasted sesame seeds for garnish

Gochujang to taste

**TIP:**
Bibimbap means "mix rice." So, before you eat, mix everything up.

# NEW YEAR'S SOUP

Also known as *tteokguk* in Korean, this soup is a MUST in our home every New Year's Day. Our family celebrates both Korean and Japanese cultures, so we always have a mix of traditional dishes from both sides.

1. In a large pot, add the water and beef and bring it to a boil. Cook until the beef is tender, about 1 hour.

2. While you wait, slice the onion into ¼-inch (6 mm) slices.

3. When ready, remove the beef and let it cool before slicing it against the grain into bite-size pieces.

4. Lower the heat to medium, add all the remaining ingredients, except for the eggs, and cook for 10 minutes. Turn off the heat.

5. Whisk the eggs in a small mixing bowl and then slowly pour into the soup. Do not stir the soup. Let the eggs set for 2 minutes. They should cook from the residual heat. Serve immediately.

6 cups (1.4 L) water

8 ounces (225 g) beef brisket

1 onion

2 tablespoons (12 g) beef stock powder

Black pepper to taste

Salt to taste

12 ounces (340 g) tteok

3 large eggs

# KOREAN BIRTHDAY SOUP

*Miyeokguk* in Korean, is also known as "Birthday Soup." It's made with *miyeok*, a dried seaweed. I make sure everyone in my family gets this soup every year on their birthdays, and of course, CrunchMom had some after both Jordan and Kaiya were born.

1. Cut the beef into bite-size pieces.

2. Heat the sesame oil in a large pot on high and add the beef.

3. While you wait for it to brown, add the miyeok to a small mixing bowl and cover with water to rehydrate.

4. Once rehydrated, drain, squeeze out any excess water, and cut into bite-size pieces.

5. Lower the heat to medium. Add the miyeok and all the remaining ingredients to the pot and cook for 15–20 minutes.

12 ounces (340 g) beef brisket

1 tablespoon (15 ml) sesame oil

3 tablespoons (3 g) miyeok

6 cups (1.4 L) water

3 teaspoons (5 g) beef stock powder

Black pepper to taste

Salt to taste

4 garlic cloves, minced

½ cup (120 ml) soy sauce

# SPICY KOREAN MISO SOUP

Also known as *doenjang jjigae* in Korean, this soup is typically served with Korean BBQ. I hope you guys enjoy this hearty and savory soup as much as I do.

1. Cut the pork belly into bite-size pieces.

2. Heat a large pot on high and add everything except the miso paste. Cook for 15–20 minutes or until the pork belly is cooked through (internal temperature of 165°F [74°C]).

3. Lower the heat to medium and add the miso paste. Stir the soup until all the miso has fully dissolved.

4. Let this simmer for another 5–7 minutes and then serve, garnished with green onions.

8 ounces (225 g) pork belly

5 cups (1.2 L) water

½ cup (55 g) potato, cut into bite-size pieces

½ cup (80 g) onions, cut into bite-size pieces

½ cup (35 g) mushrooms, cut into bite-size pieces

1 jalapeño

½ cup (60 g) zucchini, cut into bite-size pieces

4 garlic cloves, minced

½ tablespoon beef stock powder

1 tablespoon (13 g) Korean chili flakes

5 tablespoons (80 g) Korean miso paste

Green onions, thinly sliced, for garnish

# EVERYTHING'S BETTER WITH
# BACON KIMCHI FRIED RICE

Bacon makes everything better. Unless you don't like bacon, then you can just leave it out. Jordan and I received a lot of requests for this recipe, so this one is especially for you all.

1. Cook the bacon in a large frying pan over medium-high heat. Once you've cooked the bacon to your liking, remove from the pan and set aside. Drain out the bacon grease, but don't wipe the pan. We want to have some of that bacon grease to help flavor the fried rice.

2. In that same frying pan, turn the heat to high and add the onion, salt, and pepper. Cook the onion till it becomes translucent. Once translucent, add the kimchi and rice. Mix and cook for about 5 minutes.

3. Now, starting in the middle of the frying pan, push the ingredients toward the outer part of the pan so it creates a hole in the middle. Crack in the eggs and scramble. Once the eggs are completely cooked, add the bacon back to the pan and mix everything together. Cook for another 5 minutes and then serve hot.

4. You can garnish with sesame oil, sesame seeds, and green onions.

12 ounces (340 g) bacon, cut into bite-size pieces

1 onion, diced

Salt to taste

Black pepper to taste

3 cups (300 g) kimchi, cut into bite-size pieces

4 cups (744 g) cooked rice

3 large eggs

1 tablespoon (15 ml) sesame oil for garnish

Roasted sesame seeds for garnish

Green onions, thinly sliced, for garnish

# SIZZLING PORK BELLY KIMCHI

This dish is terrific as is, or it can be paired with rice, on top of noodles, or even sandwiched between bread (sweet rolls are awesome).

1. Heat a large frying pan on high and add the sesame oil.

2. Add the pork belly and season with pepper, beef stock powder, and soy sauce.

3. Cook for about 8 minutes or until the pork belly is no longer pink. Once the pork belly is nicely browned, add the kimchi and mix well.

4. Cook until the kimchi becomes slightly translucent and then serve, garnished with sesame seeds.

1 tablespoon (15 ml) sesame oil

16 ounces (455 g) pork belly, cut into bite-size pieces

Black pepper to taste

¼ teaspoon beef stock powder

1½ tablespoons (25 ml) soy sauce

8 ounces (225 g) kimchi, cut into bite-size pieces

Roasted sesame seeds for garnish

# KIMCHI JJIGAE
## (KIMCHI STEW)

This is a classic Korean stew that's jam-packed with huge flavors. I feel like this tastes best with a more sour kimchi, which has been fermented longer. So, whenever we have a tub of kimchi that's been in our fridge for a while, I'll throw it into a pot and make this *jjigae*.

12 ounces (340 g) pork belly

1 onion

2 teaspoons beef stock powder

2 tablespoons (20 g) minced garlic

2 tablespoons (28 ml) sesame oil

4 cups (400 g) kimchi, cut into bite-size pieces

3½ cups (825 ml) water

16 ounces (455 g) tofu, cut into ½-inch (1.3 cm) slices

Green onions, thinly sliced, for garnish

Roasted sesame seeds for garnish

Korean chili flakes, optional

1. Cut the pork belly into ¼-inch (6 mm) thick slices.

2. Heat a large pot on high. Once the pot is hot, carefully add in the pork belly and brown it on both sides (about 3–4 minutes each side).

3. Cut the onion in half, then cut that half into another half, and then cut those pieces into half again.

4. Add the onion into the pot along with the beef stock powder, garlic, sesame oil, and kimchi. Let this cook for 3–5 minutes.

5. Now, add the water and bring it to a boil. Boil on high for 3–5 minutes and then add the tofu and lower the heat to low and cover with a lid. Cook for 5 more minutes on low and then it's ready.

6. Garnish with green onions and sesame seeds. Add Korean chili flakes if you'd like some more heat.

# SWEET TTEOKBOKKI

Sweet *tteokbokki*, or simmered rice cakes, is one of my family's favorite dishes. It's sweet and savory, and if you love *tteok* (rice cakes) and *eomuk* (fish cakes) this dish is for you.

1. In a large frying pan, combine the water, soy sauce, and sugar. Bring to a boil.

2. Once the sugar is dissolved, add all the remaining ingredients and cook until the tteok has a bouncy texture.

3. Garnish with green onions and sesame seeds and serve hot.

4 cups (946 ml) water

½ cup (120 ml) soy sauce

¾ cup (150 g) sugar

½ cup (60 g) sliced zucchini, cut into half-moon shapes

½ cup (58 g) thinly sliced onions

8 ounces (225 g) eomuk

32 ounces (907 g) tteok

Green onions, thinly sliced, for garnish

Roasted sesame seeds for garnish

**TIP:**
All you spice lovers, go check out CrunchDad's Go-To Tteokbokki on page 82.

# CRUNCHDAD'S GO-TO TTEOKBOKKI

If you know me, you know that I love spicy foods. This classic Korean dish is no exception. I always make sure to have some tteok in the freezer at home, so whenever I need a dinner idea, this is my go-to.

1 onion, thinly sliced

8 tablespoons (104 g) sugar

4 tablespoons (88 g) gochujang

2 teaspoons beef stock powder

5 cups (1.2 L) water

2 pounds (900 g) tteok

12 ounces (340 g) eomuk (or another protein of choice)

Green onions, thinly sliced, for garnish

Roasted sesame seeds for garnish

1. Heat a large frying pan on high. Add the onion, sugar, gochujang, beef stock powder, and water and bring to a boil.

2. Boil for 5 minutes and then lower the heat to medium and add in the tteok and eomuk.

3. Cook on medium for 5–8 minutes or until you reach your desired consistency and the rice cakes go from stiff to bouncy.

4. Turn off the heat and garnish with the green onions and sesame seeds. This is best served hot.

**TIP:**
If you can handle the heat, just add extra gochujang for more fire.

# TWICE-FRIED K.F.C., A.K.A. KOREAN FRIED CHICKEN

When I say K.F.C., I'm not talking about a colonel, I'm talking about Korean Fried Chicken. Korean fried chicken is lighter and crispier. You can add different flavors and spices to this recipe or eat it as is.

1. Place the chicken wings into a large mixing bowl. Add all the remaining ingredients and coat the chicken.

2. In a large pot, add the oil until it's 2 inches (5 cm) deep. Heat the oil to 350°F (180°C) and cook the chicken wings until they start to float. Try to cook the wings in batches so you don't overcrowd the pot, which will reduce the heat of the oil.

3. Next, raise the heat to high. Then, fry the chicken for the second time. The chicken will be done once its internal temperature reaches 165°F (74°C).

4 pounds (1.8 kg) chicken wings

½ cup (96 g) potato starch or (65 g) cornstarch

⅔ cup (83 g) all-purpose flour

¼ teaspoon black pepper

1 tablespoon (9 g) garlic powder

1 tablespoon (7 g) onion powder

1 teaspoon baking soda

1 large egg

Neutral oil for deep-frying

**TIP:**
You can even use the sauce from our Sweet and Spicy Cauliflower recipe on page 32 to coat the chicken.

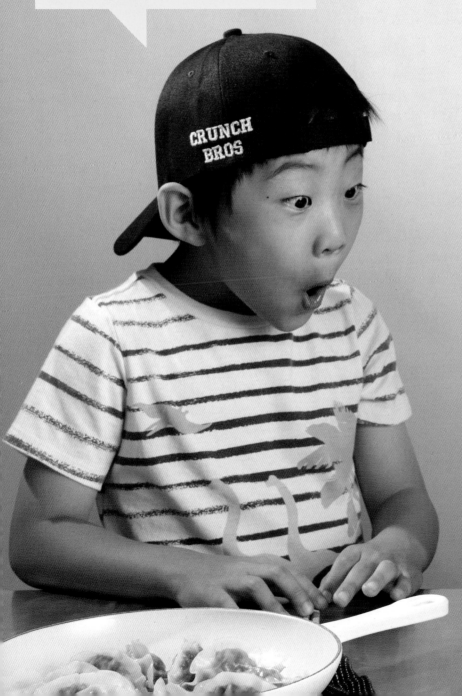

# CHECK IT OUT.

# B.C.P.
## (BUTTER, CHICKEN, AND POTATO)

If you're looking for a rich indulgent dish, look no further. But if you're counting your calories, I'd move onto the next recipe. This is a hearty dish that's best eaten over a bowl of rice.

1. Heat a large frying pan on high. Add the butter and the chicken and let the chicken brown.

2. While the chicken is cooking, cut the potatoes and carrots into 1-inch (2.5 cm) pieces. Add them into the pan and season with salt.

3. Now, mince the garlic and add to the pan along with the Korean chili flakes. Lower the heat to medium-low and cook for 25–30 minutes, stirring every few minutes.

4. Cook until the chicken has fully cooked through (internal temperature of 165°F [74°C]).

8 tablespoons (112 g) butter

32 ounces (905 g) chicken, cut into 2-inch (5 cm) pieces

3 large potatoes

3 medium carrots

Salt to taste

4 garlic cloves

3 tablespoons (39 g) Korean chili flakes

**TIP:**
You can use any cut of chicken for this recipe.

# GALBI HAMBURGER STEAK

This is not your typical hamburger. We usually eat these with a side of rice and some veggies. But they're also pretty great slapped in between a hamburger bun.

32 ounces (905 g) ground beef

½ cup (56 g) panko

1 large egg

¼ cup (40 g) diced onions

1 cup (235 ml) Galbi Marinade (see recipe on page 46)

Neutral oil for frying

Cooked rice, for serving (optional)

1. In a large mixing bowl, add the ground beef, panko, egg, onions, and ½ cup (120 ml) of Galbi Marinade and mix well.

2. Once all the ingredients are incorporated, roll the mixture into 4-ounce (115 g) meatballs.

3. Now, flatten the meatballs until you get ½-inch (1.3 cm) thick patties. Place all the patties into the freezer for 10–15 minutes. This will help keep their shape during cooking.

4. Heat a large frying pan on high. Add some oil to the pan and add the patties (cook in batches if they don't all fit).

5. Cook for 5 minutes and then flip to cook the other side.

6. Coat each patty with a tablespoon (15 ml) of the remaining ½ cup (120 ml) of Galbi Marinade.

7. Once coated, cook for 2 minutes, flip, and let cook for another 2 minutes.

8. Remove the patties from the pan and serve with cooked rice if desired.

# JALAPEÑO GARLIC PORK

Making this dish always reminds me of my Mom. I remember her making these ribs and eating them with her as a kid. Looking back now, she was probably a big reason why my spice tolerance is so high.

1. Heat a large pot on high and add the ribs.

2. While the ribs are browning, you can dice the garlic and jalapeños. You can also leave them whole. I prefer half diced and half whole.

3. Once the ribs have browned, add the garlic, jalapeños, and soy sauce.

4. Cook on medium for 30 minutes, stirring occasionally.

3 pounds (1.4 kg) pork ribs, cut into sections

1 cup (136 g) garlic cloves

10–20 jalapeños (depending on how hot you want it)

1 cup (235 ml) low-sodium soy sauce

# SPICY TTEOK SKEWERS

I like grilling a bunch of these and serving them at parties. They're always a huge hit. For those who can't handle the heat, check out the sweet, non-spicy version of this in Jordan's chapter (on page 102).

1. Add all the ingredients for the marinade to a large mixing bowl and stir until the sugar is completely dissolved. Set aside and start skewering the tteok. It's easiest if you pan fry the tteok on medium heat for 1-2 minutes just so they get soft enough to be able to skewer. On a 6-inch (15 cm) skewer, you want to add 4 to 5 pieces of tteok. Once that's all done, coat all the skewers with the marinade.

2. Heat a large frying pan on medium. Cook the skewers, basting with any leftover marinade.

3. The skewers are done when the tteok is nice and tender and best served when hot, garnished with green onions.

16 ounces (455 g) tteok

10–12 wooden skewers, 6 inches (15 cm)

Green onions, thinly sliced, for garnish

**MARINADE**

4 tablespoons (52 g) Korean chili flakes

4 tablespoons (52 g) sugar

2 tablespoons (18 g) garlic powder

2 tablespoons (14 g) onion powder

1 teaspoon black pepper

2 tablespoons (28 ml) sesame oil

4 tablespoons (60 ml) soy sauce

2 tablespoons (16 g) roasted sesame seeds

# SPICY MARINATED PORK

Pork might be my favorite protein, and if it's spicy? Now we're talking.

1. In a blender, combine all the ingredients except for the pork belly and blend till smooth.

2. Add the pork belly to a large mixing bowl and massage in the marinade. Let that marinade in the fridge for 2–4 hours.

3. Cook in a large frying pan over high heat for about 5–8 minutes on each side until the pork belly reaches an internal temp of 165°F (74°C).

4. The actual cooking time will depend on the thickness of the pork belly.

**TIP:**
Enjoy this with rice or wrapped in lettuce.

¼ cup (40 g) diced Asian pear (or ¾ cup [113 g] diced apples)

¼ cup (40 g) diced onions

1 teaspoon minced fresh ginger

5 garlic cloves

1 tablespoon (15 ml) soy sauce

2 tablespoons (26 g) Korean chili flakes

3 tablespoons (66 g) gochujang

3 tablespoons (45 ml) sesame oil

2 pounds (900 g) pork belly, cut into bite-size pieces

# CHAPTER 3

# JORDAN'S FAVORITE THINGS TO COOK AND EAT

3

# JORDAN'S CUCUMBER KIMCHI SALAD

Jordan loves experimenting around in the kitchen and making his own creations. He came up with this recipe one night and shared it with the family. It's quick, easy, refreshing, and he's super proud of this one (as are we).

4 Persian cucumbers

1 cup (100 g) kimchi

4 tablespoons (56 g) Japanese mayo

2 tablespoons (14 g) furikake

1. Slice the cucumbers into ½-inch (1.3 cm) thick rounds.

2. Place into a large mixing bowl and add in the kimchi, mayo, and furikake and then mix well.

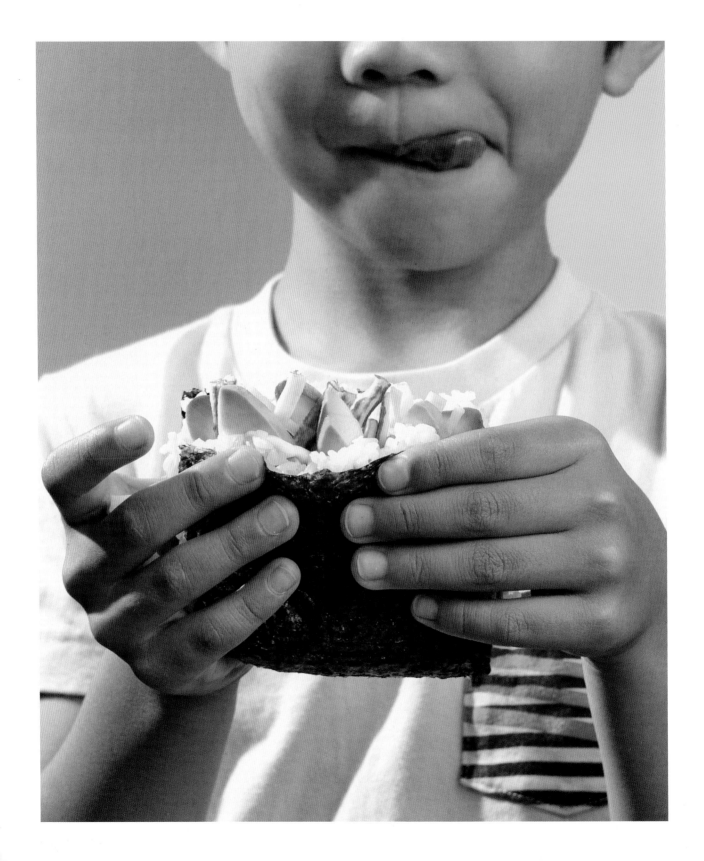

# JORDAN'S ONIGIRAZU

This is a super easy peasy version of a Japanese rice "sandwich," or *onigirazu*, that Jordan loves to make for a quick meal.

1. Cut the nori sheets in half and spread ½ cup (93 g) of the cooked rice over each piece.

2. On the right side of the sheets, add 3 slices of cucumber, then add the imitation crab on top of the cucumbers, and then 3 slices of avocado.

3. Drizzle the mayo over the avocado and fold the left side of the nori over the top.

4. Repeat for all the nori sheets.

5. Wrap them in plastic wrap and let sit for about 5 minutes before serving so that they hold their shape.

2 nori sheets

2 cups (372 g) cooked rice

1 Persian cucumber, thinly sliced

5 ounces (140 g) imitation crab, or about 6–8 sticks

1 avocado, thinly sliced

2 tablespoons (28 g) Japanese mayo

# MOCHI PIZZA

We started off experimenting with yeast and proofing, but ultimately condensed it down to this super easy recipe where you just throw everything into one bowl. Jordan and Kaiya can't get enough of this one!

1. Add all the ingredients for the dough to a large mixing bowl and mix until fully combined, about 5 minutes or until smooth.

2. Shape into 2 even balls.

3. Oil a pizza tray or cookie sheet. Flatten out the dough. Try to make it as thin as possible for a crispier crust. The thicker it is, the more chewy it will be.

4. Prebake the dough at 450°F (230°C, or gas mark 8) for 5 minutes.

5. Take the dough out of the oven and add the sauce, mozzarella cheese, and desired toppings.

6. Bake again at 450°F (230°C, or gas mark 8) for 10 minutes or until the bottom is crispy. Note that after baking, the center of the pizza dough will look almost translucent. Don't worry, it's not raw—it's mochi!

**TIP:**
Experiment with all different types of toppings and cheeses.

## DOUGH

½ cup (63 g) all-purpose flour

1 cup (160 g) mochiko

¼ teaspoon sugar

½ teaspoon salt

1 tablespoon (15 ml) olive oil

¾ cup (175 ml) water

## TOPPINGS

6 tablespoons (90 g) pizza sauce, (90 g) marinara sauce, (90 g) ketchup, or (96 g) BBQ sauce

1½ cups (175 g) shredded mozzarella cheese (or your favorite cheese blend)

Any additional desired toppings such as vegetables or cooked meats

# SWEET TTEOK SKEWERS

Jordan loves all things mochi and all things tteok. These sweet tteok skewers are a family favorite, and they disappear super quick. Plus, everything tastes better on a stick, right?

1 pound (455 g) tteok

8–10 wooden skewers, 6 inches (15 cm)

Green onions, thinly sliced, for garnish

## MARINADE

4 tablespoons (52 g) sugar

2 tablespoons (18 g) garlic powder

2 tablespoons (14 g) onion powder

2 tablespoons (28 ml) sesame oil

4 tablespoons (60 ml) soy sauce

2 tablespoons (16 g) roasted sesame seeds

1. Add all the ingredients for the marinade to a large mixing bowl and mix until the sugar is completely dissolved.

2. Set aside and start skewering the tteok. It's easiest if you pan fry the tteok on medium heat for 1-2 minutes just so they get soft enough to be able to skewer. On a 6-inch (15 cm) skewer, you want to add 4 to 5 pieces of tteok.

3. Coat all the skewers with the marinade.

4. Heat a large frying pan on medium and cook the skewers, basting with any leftover marinade. The skewers are done when the tteok is nice and tender and best served when hot, garnished with green onions.

**TIP:**

We use gyoza wrappers, but if you can't find them, other dumpling wrappers will work too. Just note, the bigger the wrapper, the more filling you'll need to put into the center of the dumpling.

# GALBI GYOZA

Jordan's Auntie gave us the suggestion to make these delicious Japanese dumplings, or *gyoza*, and then the idea just grew. Working on it together, we came up with one of *the* most tasty dumplings. They're so flavorful, you won't need a dipping sauce.

1. In a large mixing bowl, thoroughly combine all the ingredients for the filling and then set aside.

2. In a separate mixing bowl, mix all the ingredients for the marinade and pour it into the filling mixture. Stir to combine and let marinate for about 10 minutes.

3. Next, take a gyoza wrapper and place about ¾ tablespoon of the filling mixture into the center of the wrapper. Dip a finger in a small bowl of water and wet the inside perimeter of the wrapper. This will act like a glue that holds the gyoza together.

4. There are a few ways you can fold these, but this is the way we like to do it. Carefully bring up one side of the wrapper and fold over to the other side and make sure the sides are pressed tightly. Gently flatten the bottom of the dumpling so that it's standing upright. Continue this process until all the filling mixture is used. You should make about three dozen dumplings total.

5. Heat a large frying pan on medium to medium-high and add the oil. Place the gyozas upright into the pan. Cook for about 3–4 minutes. Then, pour about ¼ cup (60 ml) of water all around the pan and cover with a lid. Steam for about 5 minutes and enjoy hot.

## FILLING

½ pound (225 g) ground beef

¼ package tofu (about 3.5 ounces, or 100 g)

¼ cup (25 g) minced green onions

¼ cup (23 g) minced cabbage

½ tablespoon minced garlic

¼ teaspoon minced fresh ginger

## GYOZA

1 package (10 ounces, or 280 g) gyoza wrappers

2 tablespoons (28 ml) neutral oil

¼ cup (60 ml) water, for steaming

## MARINADE

2 tablespoons (28 ml) soy sauce

1½ tablespoons (20 g) sugar

1 teaspoon cooking sake

1 tablespoon (15 ml) sesame oil

½ teaspoon black pepper

# TUNA MAYO MINI RICE BALLS

Jordan ranked his top three favorite *onigiris*, or rice balls, and this one was one of them. The last time I made these tuna mayo balls, the kids finished off the entire plate before I finished cleaning up.

1. In a large mixing bowl, mix the tuna, mayo, salt, and pepper.

2. Add in the cooked rice, furikake, and the sheet of nori that's been ripped up into small bits. (I usually keep folding in half and tearing until I can't fold it anymore.)

3. Mix well and then divide up the rice into 8 sections.

4. Form each section into a round ball.

1 can (5 ounces, or 142 g) tuna, drained

2½ tablespoons (35 g) Japanese mayo

Salt and black pepper to taste

2 cups (372 g) cooked rice

4 tablespoons (28 g) furikake

1 nori sheet, ripped into small pieces

# BEEFY CORN FRIED RICE

Who doesn't love an easy-peasy fried rice recipe? Whenever Jordan posts recipes on his page, his amazing followers often message us saying how they made it and loved it. This fried rice dish just might be one of his most popular ones yet!

1. Heat a large frying pan on high and add the oil.

2. Add the rib eye and once it starts browning, add in the onion and the corn.

3. Cook for 3–4 minutes and then add the rice and cook for about 1 minute, mixing the rib eye and veggies together.

4. Then, add in the Yakiniku Sauce.

5. Start mixing everything together and cook until the onion is translucent (4–5 minutes). Garnish with green onions.

1–2 tablespoons (15 to 28 ml) neutral oil

1 pound (455 g) thinly sliced rib eye

1 medium onion, thinly sliced

1 can (7.5 ounces, or 215 g) corn, drained

3 cups (558 g) cooked rice

⅓ cup (80 ml) Yakiniku Sauce (see recipe on page 51)

Green onions, thinly sliced, for garnish

**TIP:**
Top it with a fried egg to take it up another level.

# MISO YAKI ONIGIRI

Onigiri are great as they are, but grilling, or *yaki* in Japanese, takes these hand-shaped rice balls up to another level. The smell of miso when it's cooking will put a smile on your face. It definitely puts a smile on Jordan's.

2 cups (372 g) cooked rice

1½ teaspoons mirin

1½ tablespoons (24 g) miso

1 tablespoon (15 ml) neutral oil

1. Form the rice into 4 triangle shapes. For this preparation, triangles work best, but you can use other shapes as well. Make sure the rice is packed tightly or they'll fall apart.

2. Mix the mirin and miso together in a small mixing bowl.

3. Heat a large frying pan on medium-low and add the oil.

4. Add the onigiri and cook on one side for 1–2 minutes. Flip and baste with the miso paste.

5. Once the bottom is crispy, flip and then do the other sides. Do not cook the miso for too long because it burns quickly.

# JORDAN'S FAMOUS OKONOMIYAKI

This savory Japanese pancake was the recipe that Jordan made when he was a special guest on *The Rachael Ray Show*. It was such a cool experience, and he did such an awesome job. We say this often, but we're so proud of our little guy.

1. Whisk together the flour, eggs, and water in a large mixing bowl until the lumps are gone. Mix in the cabbage and pork or beef.

2. Heat a large frying pan on medium and add the oil. Once the oil is hot, add a ladle of okonomiyaki batter into the pan and spread in a circle. Cook on both sides until golden brown, about 6 to 7 minutes.

3. Spread the okonomiyaki sauce over the okonomiyaki and then drizzle with mayo.

4. Sprinkle bonito flakes and aonori on top and garnish with benishouga.

5. Repeat with the remaining batter.

**TIP:**
There are no limitations on the combinations of different proteins and veggies you can use.

## OKONOMIYAKI

3¼ cups (406 g) all-purpose flour

2 large eggs

1¼ cups (285 ml) water

3 cups (210 g) chopped cabbage

1 pound (455 g) thinly sliced pork or beef

4 tablespoons (60 ml) neutral oil

## TOPPINGS

6 tablespoons (105 g) okonomiyaki sauce

4 tablespoons (56 g) Japanese mayo

Bonito flakes to taste

Aonori to taste

Benishouga to taste

# MISO MAYO UDON

This is a simple, creamy, and flavorful dish you can put together in minutes. The kids love anything with noodles and when you add corn and cucumbers, it's a done deal.

1. Boil the udon for about 8–10 minutes or until tender and then drain.

2. Meanwhile, make the sauce by combining the miso, mayo, and mentsuyu.

3. Rinse the udon and add to a large mixing bowl.

4. Add the vegetables and sauce to the udon and mix well.

3 packages frozen udon (about 26.5 ounces, or 750 g)

2 tablespoons (32 g) miso

2 tablespoons (28 g) Japanese mayo

1 tablespoon (15 ml) mentsuyu

1 cup (210 g) corn

1–2 Persian cucumbers, julienned

# WHAT SHOULD I MAKE FOR DINNER?

# KIMCHI UDON

These stir-fried noodles are a perfect mix of Jordan's Korean and Japanese side. This dish has umami as well as a little heat.

1. Boil the udon for about 5 minutes and then drain.

2. Heat a large frying pan on medium-high and add the sesame oil.

3. Add the kimchi, cook for about 3 minutes, and then add the udon, mentsuyu, and soy sauce.

4. Stir and cook for a few more minutes until everything is thoroughly coated.

5. Garnish with green onions and serve.

4 packages frozen udon (about 35 ounces, or 995 g)

1½ tablespoons (25 ml) sesame oil

2 cups (200 g) kimchi

3 tablespoons (45 ml) mentsuyu

1 teaspoon soy sauce

Green onions, thinly sliced, for garnish

# SUSHI BAKE

Here's another recipe of ours that got some fame on the Internet. We can't take credit for coming up with the original idea, but this one is our own version. This recipe is also a great option for people who don't care for raw fish or can't consume it.

1. Mix the cooked rice, sushi seasoning, and salt.

2. Press the rice into the bottom of a 9-inch × 13-inch (23 cm × 33 cm) baking dish.

3. Add the cream cheese, imitation crab, mayo, and tobiko to a large mixing bowl and combine. Spread the mixture over the rice.

4. Bake at 400°F (200°C, or gas mark 6) for 20 minutes.

5. Sprinkle furikake over the top and enjoy eating it wrapped in pieces of nori.

3 cups (558 g) cooked rice

⅓ cup (80 ml) liquid sushi seasoning

Pinch salt

8 ounces (225 g) cream cheese

1 cup (170 g) diced imitation crab

1 cup (224 g) Japanese mayo

3 tablespoons (48 g) tobiko

Furikake for garnish

Nori sheets, for serving

**TIP:**
You can also incorporate salmon, real crabmeat, and other types of seafood into this dish.

# IN THE KITCHEN WITH CRUNCHMOM

4

# RAMEN SALAD

I absolutely love this salad, as does the rest of the CrunchFam. I make big batches of it whenever we have picnics or go to get-togethers. Everyone will be coming to you for the recipe once you share this one.

1. Crush up the bag of ramen. Open it up and take out the seasoning packet and set aside.

2. Place the cabbage and green onions into a large serving bowl and add the crushed ramen and almonds.

3. In a separate bowl, thoroughly combine all the ingredients for the dressing and immediately pour onto the salad.

4. Drain the can of mandarin oranges and place them on top.

**TIP:**
After crushing the ramen, you can pan fry (no oil) to make it crispy.

1 package (3 ounces, or 85 g) ramen (I usually use beef flavor.)

½ head cabbage (about 1 pound, or 455 g), cut into ½-inch (1.3 cm) pieces

3 green onion stalks, thinly sliced

½ cup (46 g) toasted sliced almonds

1 can (15 ounces, or 425 g) mandarin oranges

**DRESSING**

2 tablespoons (28 ml) sesame oil

Ramen seasoning packet

¼ cup (60 ml) neutral oil

1½ tablespoons (20 g) sugar

½ teaspoon black pepper

Pinch salt or to taste

# J-STYLE NAPOLITAN SPAGHETTI

Napolitan pasta is a popular Japanese spaghetti dish that's also known as "ketchup spaghetti." Whenever I go back and visit Japan, I always have to make sure that I have this as one of my meals. But until I'm able to fly over, this recipe is a great alternative.

1. Bring a large pot of water to a boil and cook the pasta until al dente.

2. Drain, saving a couple of tablespoons (28 ml) of the pasta water in case you need to add it at the end.

3. Heat a large frying pan on medium-high and add the oil.

4. Add the arabiki and cook for 1–2 minutes.

5. Add the onion, mushrooms, and bell pepper. Cook until the onion becomes slightly translucent.

6. Add in the milk, ketchup, and soy sauce and mix well.

7. Add in the spaghetti and salt and pepper to taste and then mix until everything is combined.

8. Add the reserved pasta water if the dish is too dry.

9. Serve with grated Parmesan cheese.

1 pound (455 g) spaghetti

1 tablespoon (15 ml) neutral oil

½ cup (69 g) thinly sliced arabiki sausage

1 medium onion, thinly sliced

½ cup (35 g) thinly sliced button mushrooms

1 bell pepper (preferably yellow), julienned

¼ cup (60 ml) milk

½ cup (120 g) ketchup

1 teaspoon soy sauce

Salt and black pepper to taste

Grated Parmesan cheese

# WAFU-STYLE BACON AND MUSHROOM PASTA

This *wafu* or Japanese-style pasta is a light, savory, and slightly sweet noodle dish. Make this on nights you need something quick, easy, and tasty.

1. Bring a large pot of water to a boil and cook the spaghetti until al dente and drain.

2. Heat a large frying pan on medium-high.

3. Add the bacon and cook for about 2–3 minutes.

4. Add the onion and cook for another 3 minutes.

5. Then, add the mushrooms and cook for about 1 minute. Add in the spaghetti. Add the mentsuyu and mirin and mix until everything is combined. Cook until most of the liquid is gone.

6. Garnish with green onions and shredded nori.

1 package (17.6 ounces, or 500 g) spaghetti

5 slices bacon, cut into ¼-inch (6 mm) pieces

1 medium onion, thinly sliced

2 cups (140 g) thinly sliced mushrooms

½ cup (120 ml) mentsuyu

3 tablespoons (45 ml) mirin

Green onions, thinly sliced, for garnish

Shredded nori for garnish

# BABA'S EGGPLANT

Baba introduced this recipe to us a while back, and now this is the only way we ever prepare eggplant at home. The Japanese eggplants are longer and thinner than most other varieties of eggplants.

1. Cut the eggplant into about ½-inch (1.3 cm) thick circles.

2. Place the eggplant slices into a large mixing bowl and cover with the potato starch, making sure to coat each piece.

3. Heat a large frying pan on medium-high and add a generous amount of oil so the whole pan is covered.

4. Lay the eggplant slices onto the pan so they're in a single layer and cook on both sides until they get slightly tender (about 4–5 minutes each side). If your pan isn't large enough, cook in batches.

5. Mix all the ingredients for the sauce together.

6. Remove the pan from the heat and add the sauce, making sure all the slices get thoroughly coated.

3–4 Japanese eggplants, about 1 pound (455 g)

3 tablespoons (36 g) potato starch

Neutral oil for frying

**SAUCE**

3 tablespoons (45 ml) soy sauce

1½ tablespoons (20 g) sugar

1½ tablespoons (25 ml) mirin

**TIP:**
You can substitute cornstarch for the potato starch if you don't have any on hand.

# EASY SALMON RICE

Do you need a light and healthy meal? This one's for you. I always like making this dish for Jordan and Kaiya after we've had a few days of eating out or doing mukbangs.

1 pound (455 g) salmon

5 tablespoons (75 ml) liquid sushi seasoning

4 cups (744 g) cooked rice

2 tablespoons (12 g) minced fresh ginger

Shredded nori

1. Bake, panfry, or air fry the salmon.

2. Once it's done, break the salmon up into tiny pieces.

3. In a large mixing bowl, mix the sushi seasoning with the rice.

4. Add the flaked salmon and ginger and stir to combine.

5. Garnish with shredded nori.

**TIP:**
I usually leave the ginger off to the side when I make this just because sometimes it's a little too spicy for the kids.

# MISOYAKI SALMON

This *misoyaki*, or miso-grilled, salmon dish is a must try for all salmon lovers. It pairs best with rice and a bowl of miso soup.

2 tablespoons (32 g) miso

1½ tablespoons (20 ml) mirin

½ tablespoon sugar

1 pound (455 g) salmon

1. Mix the miso, mirin, and sugar together then set aside 1 tablespoon (15 ml) for basting later. Rub the remaining miso mixture all over the salmon.

2. Let it marinate in the fridge for a few hours or overnight.

3. Scrape off the excess miso.

4. Bake the salmon at 350°F (180°C, or gas mark 4) for about 10 minutes or until fully cooked.

5. Then, take the salmon out and rub it with the remaining miso mixture.

6. Return to the oven and bake for another 5 minutes.

# PANKO AND TARTAR SAUCE SALMON

This is a fun salmon recipe that the kids love. It's a little crunchy, it's a little creamy, and the pickles add a nice touch.

1. Pat down and dry the salmon.

2. Oil a baking tray and place the salmon on top.

3. Sprinkle with salt and pepper and then coat with the tartar sauce.

4. Add the pickles and panko on top and then drizzle with olive oil.

5. Bake at 400°F (200°C, or gas mark 6) for about 15–20 minutes or until the fish is fully cooked.

1 pound (455 g) salmon

Salt and black pepper

3 tablespoons (45 g) tartar sauce

2 pickle spears, minced

3 tablespoons (21 g) panko

1–1½ tablespoons (15 to 20 ml) olive oil

SERVES 3–4

# TOFU AND CHICKEN HAMBAGU

These Japanese-style "hamburger steaks" are a family favorite that was introduced to us by Baba, and we went nuts over them. We usually serve these with a side of rice and veggies.

1. In a large mixing bowl, combine the tofu, ground chicken, panko, cornstarch, sugar, chicken bouillon powder, ginger, salt, and pepper. Mix well and form the mixture into small round patties about ½-inch (1.3 cm) thick.

2. Heat a large frying pan on medium-high and add 2 tablespoons (28 ml) of oil.

3. Add the patties and cook for about 5–7 minutes. Flip the patties and then cover them and let cook until cooked through, about 5–7 minutes more.

4. Mix all the ingredients for the sauce together.

5. Lower the heat to medium-low and add the sauce around the pan. Cook until the sauce is caramelized, making sure to flip the patties so both sides are evenly covered.

**TIP:**
Cook in batches if you don't have a pan large enough for all of the patties at once.

14 ounces (390 g) tofu, drained

1½ pounds (680 g) ground chicken

½ cup (56 g) panko

5 tablespoons (40 g) cornstarch

3 teaspoons (13 g) sugar

¼ teaspoon chicken bouillon powder

½ teaspoon grated fresh ginger

Pinch salt

Pinch black pepper

2 tablespoons (28 ml) neutral oil

## SAUCE

3 tablespoons (45 ml) soy sauce

3 tablespoons (45 ml) mirin

3 tablespoons (45 ml) cooking sake

3 tablespoons (39 g) sugar

# SWEET AND TANGY EBI

*Ebi*, the word for shrimp in Japanese, is Kaiya's favorite seafood dish. The kids are always happy when it's ebi night.

1. Mix all the ingredients for the sauce together.

2. Heat a large frying pan on medium-high and add the oil.

3. Add the onion, garlic, and ginger into the pan and cook until the onion is translucent.

4. Add the ebi and when it turns pink, add in the sauce.

5. Stir to combine and cook for about 2 minutes.

1 tablespoon (15 ml) neutral oil

½ onion, minced

3 garlic cloves minced

1 tablespoon (6 g) minced fresh ginger

12 ounces (340 g) ebi

**SAUCE**

4 tablespoons (60 g) ketchup

2 teaspoons soy sauce

2 teaspoons cooking sake

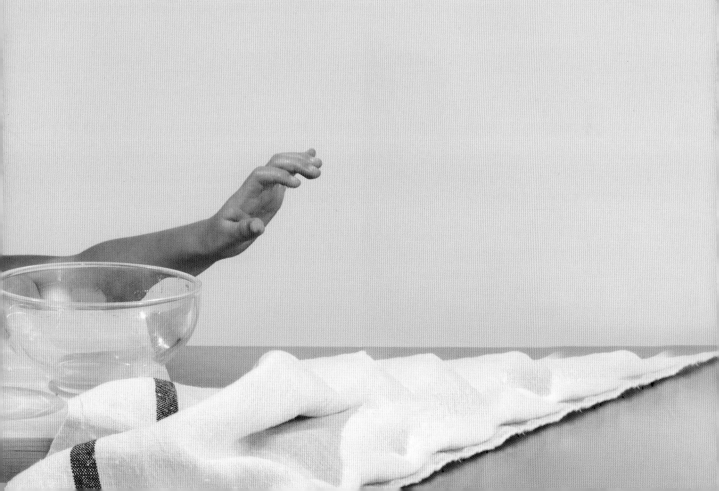

KAIYA'S IN THE KITCHEN!

# CRUNCHMOM AND BABA'S OYAKODON

Here's Baba and my take on this classic Japanese dish. *Oyako* means "parent and child," so it was serendipitous that we came up with this recipe together.

1. In a small mixing bowl, mix all the ingredients for the sauce until the sugar is fully dissolved.

2. Cut the chicken into bite-size pieces.

3. Heat a large frying pan on medium-high and add the oil.

4. Add the chicken and cook for about 4–5 minutes.

5. Add the onion and cook for about 5 minutes or until the onion becomes translucent.

6. Pour the sauce into the pan and cook until it's reduced to about half and the chicken is cooked through.

7. Then, whisk the eggs and pour it over the pan.

8. Lower the heat to medium and cover the pan until the eggs are done to your liking.

9. Scoop over a bowl of rice and garnish with shredded nori and benishouga.

1 pound (455 g) boneless chicken thighs or breasts

1 onion, thinly sliced

1 tablespoon (15 ml) neutral oil

5 large eggs

Cooked rice for serving

Shredded nori for garnish

Benishouga for garnish

### SAUCE

½ tablespoon dashi powder

½ cup (60 ml) warm water

4 teaspoons (16 g) sugar

2 tablespoons (28 ml) mirin

3 tablespoons (45 ml) soy sauce

# BABA'S GARLIC SHOYU CHICKEN

This is one of Baba's signature dishes I remember eating growing up. She passed the recipe down to me, and now we make it all the time for Jordan and Kaiya. We like to eat this with a side of rice and fresh veggies like our shoyu mayo asparagus, on page 35.

1. Place the chicken thighs in a lidded container.

2. Combine all the ingredients for the marinade and pour it over the chicken.

3. Let it marinate in the fridge for 3–4 hours.

4. Heat a large frying pan on medium-high and add the oil.

5. Cook the chicken until golden brown. Then, flip the chicken over and turn the heat to medium or medium-low.

6. Cover the pan with a lid and cook for about 10 minutes.

7. Remove the lid and flip the chicken for 1–2 minutes or until the chicken is fully cooked (internal temperature of 165°F [74°C]).

1½ pounds (680 g) chicken thighs

1 tablespoon (15 ml) neutral oil

**MARINADE**

3 tablespoons (45 ml) soy sauce

2 tablespoons (28 ml) mirin

3–4 garlic cloves, grated

1½ teaspoons onion powder

# EVERYONE'S FAVORITE SUKIYAKI

You can eat *sukiyaki* any time of year, but all of my memories of eating this dish is in the winter. We always put a big electric skillet in the center of the table while we'd all sit around and eat it family style.

1. Bring a large pot of water to a boil and cook the shirataki for 3–4 minutes. Drain and set aside.

2. Heat a large frying pan on medium-high and add the oil.

3. Add the beef and cook until browned.

4. Add all the veggies, tofu, and shirataki, making sure to put them into their own sections in the pan.

5. In a small mixing bowl, combine the sake, sugar, and mentsuyu soy sauce and then pour it over the ingredients in the pan. Make sure to distribute it all around.

6. Cover the pan and cook for 15–20 minutes or until the veggies are tender, stirring occasionally but making sure to keep all the ingredients in their own section.

**TIP:**
Traditionally, sukiyaki is made with all of the ingredients in their own sections, but you can mix it all around if preferred.

1 tablespoon (15 ml) neutral oil

14 ounces (390 g) shirataki

1½ pounds (680 g) thinly sliced beef

15–20 napa cabbage leaves, cut into 1-inch (2.5 cm) pieces

10 green onion stalks (about 5.5 ounces, or 155 g), cut into 2-inch (5 cm) pieces

⅔ cup (100 g) mushrooms of choice, like shiitake or enoki

1 package (14 ounces, or 390 g) medium–firm tofu, cut evenly into 8 cubes

⅓ cup (80 ml) soy sauce

½ cup (120 ml) cooking sake

6 tablespoons (78 g) sugar

¼ cup (60 ml) mentsuyu

# QUICK AND EASY NIKUJAGA

*Nikujaga*, which literally means "meat and potatoes," is one of my favorite Japanese one-pot dishes that I like to make for the family. It's hearty, and I love that you can actually make it all in one pot.

1. Mix all the sauce ingredients together.

2. Heat a large pot on medium and add the oil.

3. Cook the beef for about 1 minute until it starts to brown.

4. Add the potatoes, carrots, and onions.

5. Mix in the sauce and then cover for about 20–25 minutes, stirring occasionally until the potatoes are tender.

1 tablespoon (15 ml) neutral oil

1 pound (455 g) thinly sliced beef

3 medium potatoes, cut into 1-inch (2.5 cm) cubes

2 onions, sliced 1-inch (2.5 cm) thick

2 carrots, cut into ¾-inch (1.9 cm) rounds

### SAUCE

5 tablespoons (75 ml) soy sauce

2 tablespoons (26 g) sugar

1½ tablespoons (25 ml) cooking sake

1 tablespoon (15 ml) mirin

# A GLOSSARY OF
# KOREAN AND JAPANESE FOODS

**aonori** These are aromatic dried green seaweed flakes often used as garnish on dishes like *okonomiyaki*, Japanese pancakes, and *takoyaki*, seafood dumplings.

**arabiki sausages** These are fully cooked smoked Japanese sausages that have a slightly sweet and smoky flavor.

**beef stock powder** This is a commonly used stock powder in Korean cooking. It helps add umami and savoriness to dishes.

**benishouga** This is a type of Japanese pickle made of sliced ginger. It is red in color and has a slightly sour and spicy component to it from being pickled in plum vinegar.

**bibimbap** This is a popular Korean dish that means "mixing rice." It consists of a bowl of rice topped with various ingredients such as meat and vegetables.

**birthday soup** Also known as *miyeok guk* in Korean, this is a soup made with miyeok. It is eaten during times of celebration such as birthdays and also given to women after giving birth.

**black bean paste** Also known in Korean as *jjajang*, this is fermented black soybean paste most commonly used in a dish called *Jjajangmyeon* or "black bean noodles."

**bonito flakes** Known as *katsuobushi* in Japanese, these are bonito fish flakes that have been dried, smoked, and fermented.

**bulgogi** This is a Korean dish of thinly sliced meat that's been marinated in a soy sauce base and typically cooked over an open flame (such as a barbecue grill).

**cooking sake** This is Japanese alcohol made from fermented rice. There's a difference between cooking sake (*ryorishu*) and the sake that you drink. Cooking sake has less alcohol content and contains salt.

**daikon** This is a large, white Japanese radish that can be eaten raw, cooked, or pickled. It's called *mu* in Korean.

**dashi** This is a type of broth or soup stock, usually made from kombu (kelp) or bonito flakes.

**dashi powder** This is an umami-rich granulated soup stock flavored primarily with dried bonito. Simply add to boiling water to make dashi.

**ebi** This is the word for "shrimp" or "prawns" in Japanese.

**eomuk** These are Korean fish cakes used both in Korean and Japanese dishes. It's usually made by steaming ground fish and seafood with other ingredients to form a meat-like texture.

**furikake** This is a savory Japanese condiment that's typically used to season rice. It's ingredients include seaweed, fish flakes, sesame seeds, salt, and much more.

**galbi** This is the Korean word for "rib." The most common type of galbi is marinated beef short rib.

**gochujang** This is a sweet and spicy fermented Korean chili paste made mainly from red chile peppers, glutinous rice, soy beans, and salt. It's a popular paste to add spiciness and heat to Korean dishes.

**gyoza** These are Japanese panfried dumplings typically filled with minced pork and vegetables.

**imitation crab** Also known as *kanikama* in Japanese or *maht sal* in Korean, this is usually made from ground white fish, usually Atlantic pollock, and shaped into sticks.

**Japanese mayo** Very different from other types of mayonnaise, Japanese mayo only uses egg yolks, which makes it creamier. It also has a sweetness and tanginess to it due to the vinegar that's used.

**jjajangmyeon** This is a Chinese-Korean noodle dish that's made using black bean paste and thick and chewy wheat noodles.

**jjigae** This is the word "stew" in Korean. The most popular form of jjigae is kimchi jjigae.

**kimbap** This is a Korean dish that means "seaweed and rice." It typically contains various meats, veggies, and rice that's rolled up in a seaweed wrapper.

**kimchi** This is a fermented side dish, most commonly made with cabbage. It has tons of health benefits, such as being high in vitamins and probiotics, and is by far the most popular Korean side dish.

**Korean chili flakes** Also known as *gochugaru*, this is an essential ingredient when cooking spicy Korean foods. It's typically seedless and comes in both flake and powder form.

**liquid sushi seasoning** This is like rice vinegar, but seasoned. It's used to season sushi rice.

**mentsuyu** This is a liquid Japanese soup base used often in noodle dishes like udon and soba.

**mirin** The Japanese condiment mirin is a rice wine that's slightly similar to sake, but sweeter and with less alcohol content. It has a thicker consistency and is used a lot in sauces, glazes, and marinades.

**miso** This is a thick paste made from fermented soybeans. It's full of umami and often used in soups, dips, and marinades.

**miyeok** This is a dried edible seaweed. It's a main ingredient in Korean Birthday Soup.

**mochi** These are Japanese rice cakes made out of glutinous rice flour.

**mochiko** This is flour made from *mochigome*, which is sweet and glutinous rice often used to make mochi.

**napa cabbage** This is a type of Chinese cabbage that's widely used in Asian cuisines.

**nikujaga** A popular Japanese comfort dish, the name of this stew literally means "meat and potatoes."

**nori** This is dried edible seaweed often made into sheets that can be used to wrap sushi.

**okonomiyaki** This is a savory Japanese-style pancake made of ingredients such as flour, eggs, and cabbage. It's definitely a very popular comfort food.

**onigirazu** This is a type of Japanese rice ball that resembles a sandwich. It consists of rice layered with different types of meat and veggies encased inside a sheet of nori.

**onigiri** These are Japanese rice balls typically shaped as triangles. They come with various fillings in the center and are oftentimes wrapped with nori.

**oyakodon** This classic Japanese dish means "parent and child." It's a dish made of chicken and eggs simmered in broth and served over a bed of rice.

**panko** These are Japanese breadcrumbs often used to coat deep-fried foods.

**potato starch** Known as *katakuriko* in Japanese, it's a powdered starch similar to cornstarch.

**rice cakes** These are also known as *tteok* in Korean and *mochi* in Japanese. They're made by steaming rice flour and other glutinous flours and then mixing it with water and forming the mixture into various shapes. The most popular Korean dish using this ingredient is tteokbokki.

**rice vinegar** This is a vinegar made from fermented rice, often used as a seasoning in dressings and dips.

**shirataki** These are Japanese noodles made from the konjac yam. They're long and white and have a bouncy texture.

**somen** This is a type of Japanese noodle that's thin, white, made of wheat flour, and often eaten cold.

**takuwan** This is the name for pickled daikon in Japanese. It's called *danmuji* in Korean. The most popular ones you can find are bright yellow in color.

**tobiko** This bright orange flying fish roe is considered a delicacy in Japan. It's often used as a topping for crab cakes, sushi, and other seafood dishes.

**tteok** These are Korean rice cakes made from steamed rice flour.

**tteokbokki** This means "stir-fried rice cake" in Korean. Considered a comfort food, it's a really popular street food that's sweet and spicy.

**tteokguk** This Korean rice cake soup is also known as "New Year's Soup." You eat this on the first day of the Lunar New Year to signify the beginning of a new year and good fortune. This soup's main ingredient is tteok.

**udon** This is a type of Japanese noodle that's thick, white, and made of wheat flour. It has a soft and chewy consistency.

**yakiniku** This also means "grilled meat" in Japanese. It's most commonly known as meat cooked over a charcoal grill and served with a yakiniku dipping sauce.

# ABOUT THE AUTHORS

**JEFF AND JORDAN KIM** are the much-beloved, wildly popular, incredibly endearing, and subtly funny father-son duo known as The CrunchBros. In their first three years, they gathered more than 3.9 million followers on TikTok, YouTube, and Instagram, with many of their videos earning more than a half million likes each. And what do the Bros do? It's simple: They cook, eat, and learn about food, mainly Korean-inspired favorites from dad Jeff's Korean background and Japanese-inspired dishes from the culinary heritage of the behind-the-scenes, off-camera CrunchMom, also known as CrunchBoss. The Bros get thousands of fan messages from young and old alike, especially from parents who say The CrunchBros videos have motivated their children to try new foods and develop a more adventuresome palate. The CrunchBros have been featured on Buzzfeed, Rachael Ray, Tasty, and Food Network, among other venues. They live with little-sister Kaiya and, of course, CrunchMom, in Orange County, California, just south of Los Angeles.

# ACKNOWLEDGMENTS

**Baba:** Thank you for your unconditional love. Thank you for your patience and for putting up with us while we jumped into all of this. You have been such a huge inspiration in so many of our recipes, especially for Jordan and CrunchMom. Thank you for all the hours you watched the kids so we could get work done. This would not have been possible if it were not for you. Thank you, Baba. We love you.

**Kat Lieu:** You were the motivation for us to start this book and now we've come full circle to have you be a part of it with us. Thank you for always being an inspiration and for your friendship that started from that first day Subtle Asian Baking reached out to us.

**David Peng:** We don't know how we could have done this without you. It was an intense few days, but there's no other team we would have been happier going through it with. Words cannot express how thankful we are for you and your talents. The photographs all came out incredibly. Now, let's go eat!

**Christiane Hur:** Watching you work your magic was incredible. Thank you for bringing our dishes to life and for sharing your food-styling skills and talents with us. The Dream Team!

**Chanteal Takeuchi:** Thank you for all your hard work on the shoot. We couldn't agree more when you said it didn't feel like we were going to work, but it was more like hanging out with family.

**Sally and Stacey Kim:** Words can never express how grateful we are for the two of you. We appreciate all of the input you had on this book and we thank you for the suggestions you made and for testing out our recipes. Also, most importantly, for being some of the best aunties our kids could ever ask for.

**Chef Barb:** We don't know how we got so lucky to have crossed paths with you, but we are so grateful that we did. Thank you for being such a positive light in our world.

**Chef Trevor:** We're so honored to have you be a part of this project with us. Much respect and mahalo. We can't wait to see you back on the island.

**Christina Jira:** To say that we are eternally grateful for our friendship is an understatement. Thank you for letting us lean on you for advice and for the many hours you put into helping us with the vision for our book.

**Hugh Harper:** Thank you for convincing CrunchMom to put herself into this book.

Thank you to our publishing team at Quarto. We hit the ground running with this project. Thank you for believing in us from Day One.

A special thank you to our friends and family who have supported us and have been by our side unconditionally. Thank you to all our recipe testers, our babysitters, and our fellow foodies.

Writing a cookbook was one of the toughest projects we have taken on. It was an emotional roller coaster from start to finish, but it has become one of our most rewarding accomplishments. This cookbook was a labor of love from and for our family and it was only made possible because of you. Thank you all.

# INDEX